AMAZON FBA BLUEPRINT

AMAZON FBA BLUEPRINT: HOW TO LAUNCH A PRIVATE-LABEL EMPIRE, BUILD A SIX-FIGURE PASSIVE INCOME AND ACHIEVE FINANCIAL FREEDOM

By

CRAIG LEBOWSKI

Copyright © 2016

LEGAL NOTES

INTRODUCTION

There has been much said and written about Amazon as a company and the opportunities that they offer people to make a living. Amazon is a global phenomenon that has gone from a company that didn't know how to make a profit to something that has made people rich the world over. But how does this happen? Well Amazon are in many markets all over the world and they use their website and the way it is structured to generate sales for itself but also gives you and me (the little guys) a chance to sell products on their website. This is really Amazon's response to eBay and the way that it works is that you can sell items on the Amazon Marketplace to consumers in your chosen market. If you become an Amazon Marketplace seller then you immediately open up access to the millions of Amazon buyers in your chosen markets. When a customer clicks in a product they are aware that they are buying from Amazon. What they may not know is that this product might be provided by someone other than Amazon – and this is where you come in. You can use the Amazon system to access to Amazon customers and sell products to them on a large scale and make great money by doing so. This is a great way to make a living and many thousands of people do just this all over the world. I can hear you asking yourself – just how do I become a part of this? What do I have to do to make great money from my own home? Who is going to help me to become a success by selling on Amazon? Well the answers are all here in this book. It will give you all the knowledge, information and confidence you need to be able to become a success by selling on Amazon.

This book will give you a step-by-step guide to getting set up an Amazon FBA seller and shows you how to become a success year after year. It is important to make the most of an opportunity like this so you want to do everything you can in order to make great money from Amazon and the FBA program. We will help you to understand what FBA does and how you van best make it work to your advantage.

Amazon is a company that has built up a huge number of loyal and repeat customers. They have done this over a long period of time through offering a huge range of products at great process and by knowing both their business and their customers. They carefully built up profiles of their individual customers and their customer groups and this allowed them to show their customers the products that they were fairly sure they were interested ion and had a chance of selling them. Now you as an individual seller can get in on the act. The fact is that Amazon allows individual sellers to sell their items on Amazon. Now this means that you can access all of these customers on this popular website with products of your own. The potential here is absolutely enormous and you can make your own mark in this area if you so things right. And that is where this book comes in. We look at how to start a business sin no time and how to go through the right steps to make great money from the fact that Amazon allows you to use their website and show your wares to their customers.

Amazon as a company is huge. They are valued in the hundreds of billions of dollars and this all came about because they knew exactly what they wanted to be. They knew their customers and how to tap into their customers. They knew how to grow and where to push their efforts. And you need to have a level of vision too. I'm not expecting you to turn yourself into a multi-billion dollar company. But with my help you can make very good money from this book by getting the most out of the Amazon FBA program.

But first you need to take a step. You need to become and Amazon FBA seller. Don't know what that is? Don't worry at all because that is where we will start…

CHAPTER 1

WHAT IS AMAZON FBA?

In terms of Amazon FBA stands for Fulfillment By Amazon. What this means is that you can collect up all your products and send them to an Amazon fulfillment center. Amazon has created one of the most advanced fulfillment networks in the entire world and your business can profit from their expertise. With FBA you store all of your products in an Amazon fulfillment center, and then Amazon pick, pack, ship, and provide customer service for these products. It is a great way to access a professional service for the products that you sell. When you use FBA you are tapping into a great service and network that someone else has set up. You can benefit from the hard work that Amazon has put in to being an internationally recognized company that delivers excellent products for customers at highly competitive prices with a proven track record of excellent customer service.

FBA is a way of extending your business reach. FBA is a way to make great money from Amazon. FBA is the solution if you want a great business opportunity without having to put in all the work yourself of picking, packing and delivering all of the products that you want to offer on the Amazon Marketplace. This is a great way to grow a business because it doesn't require you to have a warehouse to hold stock. It doesn't require you to hire staff to deal with customer enquiries or to send out the items as they sell. It doesn't require you to develop your own website and get it up the Google search rankings. All of this has been done for you.

Amazon FBA is a way of you finding your own niche in the market and exploiting it to make great money for yourself day after day, week after week, year after year. FBA is a program that will allow you to get the most out of the success of Amazon for yourself without getting your hands dirty! It is the formula for success because it gives you the ability to get your product out there into the market and gain more views and buyers than ever before. It gives you a privileged place on the world's biggest market place to earn a great profit that can change your lifestyle. All you need is to know how.

CHAPTER 2

BENEFITS OF FBA

FBA gives you many advantages to your business. By using the FBA channel you become a sort of partner for Amazon. As said before, the customers go on to the Amazon website and click away as though they are ordering directly from Amazon. The products are then efficiently and professionally picked and dispatched to your customer without you having to lift a finger beyond the initial process. Your products can sell to any part of the world at any time of the day or night and you will be informed by an email and some money entering your bank account. This is the ultimate sleeping investment! You just sit back and wait for the money to come in!

Another great feature of the FBA program is that you get access to the Amazon Prime customers. An Amazon Prime customer pays an annual subscription for Amazon services and as part of this program they receive free 2-day shipping on items that are dispatched by Amazon. So when you enroll in FBA all of your products automatically become a part of the Amazon Prime family. Your products can be selected by these buyers. When someone pays for the privilege of Amazon Prime then they are incredibly unlikely to select products that incur a delivery charge so being a part of the program gives you great access to the large part of the Amazon market.

The customer service aspect of all of this takes a large amount of time and pressure away from you and gives it to the trained, professional and experienced Amazon tram to deal with. This means that you can send your items to the fulfillment center and then really forget about what goes on with it. If there is an issue with delivery then Amazon will deal with it. If there is a question about the item then Amazon will deal with it. The amount of time that this saves is huge when it comes to running a business. If you sell thousands of items on Amazon then you could end up with scores of enquiries every week that all may take up quite a bit of your time. To be able to pass all of that worry, time and expense to someone else is an absolute godsend.

The fact is also that FBA gives you the opportunity to make more sales. There is no guarantee that you will get higher sales but most FBA sellers report a higher level of sales at a higher price point, and this is down to the fact that you access that Amazon Prime market again.

The alternative is picking, packing and shipping the items yourself from home or you place of work and this is less attractive to you as a seller and this will also be less attractive to your buyers. The sleek and trusted delivery process offered by Amazon will always be a more attractive proposition for buyers than someone selling stuff from their back room. This means that you access more buyers that are more willing to buy from you. This is the ultimate win-win situation. It also means that you can operate a multi-million dollar operation with very, very few staff. When you no longer need to spend your time warehousing products, picking them, packing them and finding a delivery solution your need for extra help reduces massively. I know of people that have a multi-million dollar Amazon FBA business that is run by one or two people. This is because the work is all in the ordering from a supplier and the branding of the Private Label product. Everything else is done by Amazon. They store your products. The Amazon website handles your order without you even knowing. Their staff locates your products when an order comes in. Amazon sends it out and then they handle any customer queries or returns should they happen. Once the product arrives at the Amazon fulfillment center you just wait for your bank balance to grow. You don't need to do anything else in regards handling your product or dealing with your customers. It is that easy.

The one area of Amazon that has been treasured in recent years is the Buy Box that you find on the screen on any product page. This appears with the 'preferred' seller being highlighted to the potential buyer. There are several factors at play here, and Amazon are very secretive about what exactly they are, but one major factor is the combination of price and FBA. If your competitors do not offer FBA then you have a greater chance of appearing in that box, even if your price is higher because the shipping cost will automatically be taken into account. FBA helps you win buyers in this way because you appear with a sort of 'preferred seller' status.

As you can see, there are any reasons to look at FBA for your business. The idea behind setting up a business is to make as much money as possible from as little work as possible and in this case FBA helps you on both these fronts. If you are serious about selling products on Amazon then you really need to make FBA a priority in your decision making process. Make sure that you know your stuff and that you can get everything you need in order to be a successful FBA seller on Amazon in the future. This book will look in detail at all the things you need to put together to be this successful seller.

CHAPTER 3

HOW AND WHY TO PRIVATE LABEL!

Private label takes a product and makes it unique – something of your own. In a competitive market you could go to a lot of work to source products and send them to Amazon, before you find that Amazon or other sellers have dropped the price and you are struggling to sell your stock. This happens when there are multiple sellers of the same product and you are competing for customers on price. You can end up with a lot of expensive stock sat in an Amazon fulfillment center doing nothing but gathering dust and nor generating you income. This is not what you got into this for and there us actually another way. The ideal situation is when you are selling something that nobody else does. It gives you that competitive advantage of accessing all the great FBA features outlined in the last chapter without having to compete for customers with other sellers. Private labeling involves finding products that are branded as your own. You may find a supplier that sells their product to lots of people and then these all end up on Amazon at the same time. What you want is two things. The first is for your product to stand out from the crowd. The second thing that you want is for you to be the only seller of that product. And this is where Private Labeling comes in to help you. Find a supplier that you can use that offers you the chance to have your product made differently – to be customized to your requirements. It may well be that the product is the same and does all the same things as your competitors but it will look different and will look unique. You can then sell this on Amazon using the FBA system as a different product. If you are clever with your description and your product title then you will gain sales by making your product not only appear different o the competition but better than the competition. It means that the FBA seller that can work cleverly with their supplier and make their product listing stand out will win customers and make the sales that they need without having to compete on price with similar products. When a buyer finds your product page then you will be the only seller available to them. If they want your products (and your description means that they will) then they have no option but to buy it from you.

Another way to make your own private label product is to use exactly the same product that the supplier is selling but rebrand it when it arrives in your home market. The way that your product is described on the Amazon website will help to make it stand out from the crowd when it comes to finding buyers. You will also be able to add your own packaging, your own instructions and your own logo to the product. This means that you have to get the product delivered to you and then make all of these changes before sending through to your Amazon fulfillment center but it is another way of making your product different from the rest of the market and securing you customers.

You can use this simple but really effective technique to win sales in a competitive market and increase the amount of money you make from Amazon and the FBA system. Wherever your supplier is you can simplify the process by having your products delivered directly to the Amazon fulfillment center and you don't even have to handle the products yourself as they go through the system from manufacture to customer seamlessly.

CHAPTER 4

SIGNING UP ON AMAZON FBA

The first thing you need is to sign up for an Amazon seller account. This is a simple process that you can follow on the Amazon website. If you click on the normal website for Amazon in your area then scroll to the bottom of the screen then you will find a message to click on such as 'Sell on Amazon.' When you follow this link it will take you to the part of the site where you fill in all your details and sign up with Amazon to be a registered seller with them. They will need details such as your name, your business name and address, a contact number and credit card or bank details. You will also need to provide tax details for the records that Amazon keep. There are different levels of seller and the one that you sign up for can depend on the country you are based in and the number of products that you will be selling every month. The basic level is free to sign up to and may be a good place to start the process of you are new to Amazon and want to find out what it is all about. But the seller that is really serious about all of this will need a bigger and better account so you may need to look at the options and decide which the best one for you is. You need an account that will give you the best chance of selling all the products you want and that will keep your costs to a minimum. Most of all it needs to allow you access to the Amazon FBA program because that is how you are going to leverage your investment and make great money from selling on the Amazon Marketplace.

CHAPTER 5

ESSENTIAL APPS AND TOOLS TO HELP YOU WITH FBA SUCCESS

Amazon is big money. FBA is big money too. Amazon is valued at around $175 billion and each and every one of us can get a slice of that action if you do the right things. Because there is so much money to be made with Amazon you can find it everywhere on the internet. There are Amazon FBA Facebook groups, YouTube channels, Amazon forums and much more. You could probably spend every day all day looking through them all and still not get done before you die so what is important to you? Where do you need to start looking?

This book is obviously the very first piece of information that you need. Nowhere else can you get the inside track in a step-by-step guide that will take you from an idea to a business like this. But there are other useful areas to look to get your Amazon FBA business up and running and to have all the tools you need at hand-

APPS

The first app you need is the **Amazon app**, closely followed by the **Amazon sellers app**. These will both give you access to Amazon and your selling account on the move so they are essential to keep abreast of everything that is happening with your account and Amazon in general. The clever seller knows what is going on in their market at all times so to be able to get this information at the touch of your finger is a real help in this area. There are other apps that you will find on the app store of your provider that can help you further with your FBA business and career. The more apps you read up about and try then the better informed you will be when it comes to your business. Apps will help you to work out costs, find your competitors and understand what your market sector is doing. Get armed with these on your smartphone or tablet and get ahead.

Udemy Courses

Udemy is a site where people upload quality training programs to help others, particularly with the digital economy. There are several quality courses that will help you to understand the process and give a different way of learning because the courses are very visual and contain videos. This is another way to learn.

Blogs and Forums

The advantage of blogs and forums is that they are interactive. So if you have a question you can fire way and the collective knowledge and experience of the community will give you answers or advice. You can read about many different topics and sometimes find advice that specifically relates to your situation or your market niche. Forums and blogs are able to move with the times so if there is a change in policy, a new procedure or something else happening on Amazon then you can find out all about it on one of these forum or blog websites.

Social Media

Social media is a great place to interact with other FBA sellers and share experiences. Advice is also ready to come by as people will connect and share their knowledge. It is a great community that the people who use FBA have created and generally there is a lot of love for each other. If you need help then you will find someone that is willing to give it. Social media can work like forums or blogs to keep up with the latest changes so you might want to join a Facebook groups or follow certain Twitter accounts to see what is going on and how it might affect you.

The more you learn about your chosen profession then the better you become at it. That is true for a carpenter, a lawyer and a financial advisor. And that is also true about an Amazon FBA seller. Don't close your eyes to the world around you. You have taken the first step by reading this book and the future is a path of interesting things to read and interesting people to meet. Never be afraid of that and put yourself in a position where you never think "I don't know." Always be prepared to do the research and always be prepared to get ahead of the competition. The answers are always out there and will be easier to reach than you first realize. Just get in touch with people, get reading and you will find that you become an expert in no time. Life would be boring without something new to learn!

CHAPTER 6

THE 5 PHASES OF CHOOSING A PROFITABLE PRODUCT

PHASE 1- HOW TO CHOOSE A PROFITABLE PRODUCT

Looking at the data

You need to analyze and asses the information that is available to get the right products for your FBA offering. You need to look at suppliers and the number one website that people are currently using to get products to sell on Amazon in the United States is **alibaba** in China. Alibaba is a huge Chinese company owned by Jack Ma that is full of suppliers and businesses that can help you with the right products when it comes to your FBA business. You can find a supplier for just about any consumer product so it pays to know your stuff. Because of the competitive nature of Amazon you will be best to focus on a product or product area that you know something about. When it comes to information you want to know that what you are buying suits you potential customers and give you the chance of selling large quantities to get your business off the ground and making you great money. You need to consider the Amazon fees, the shipping fees, taxes and any other costs in all your calculations because the point of this whole exercise is to make a profit. Look at all the costs associated with the purchase and sale of a product before you make any decisions.

Amazon will also give you sales rankings for products on each product page. By looking at how high something is on the Amazon sales rank you have an idea of how popular that product might be. This is important when you are making a decision on what to buy from a supplier because you want a product that will turn over quickly and generate a profit for you as soon as possible.

This type of business works on being able to sell at a profit, reinvest the money you generate and buy more items to then sell on again. The first few rounds of buying and selling come from the same money that had been recycled before you can start to pull a profit out of the business for yourself. You want and need an item that will sell through quickly so that you can reorder and start the process again.

Tracking competing products

You need to cross-reference this with what other people are doing. If you see a great product at a great price with a supplier then you need to find out what the selling process are in your chosen market. If your competitors are selling it at a price that leaves you with no profit then you will need to find another product to sell. Remember that you could get around this problem with a Private Label and some great marketing descriptions but don't leave yourself with a mountain that you cannot possible climb. Private Labeling helps to squeeze extra profit out of something that is competitive but won't overturn a massive price discrepancy against those you are competing for customers with. Don't forget that you may need to take account of currency fluctuations in your transactions so you may agree a price when the dollar to the yuan is at one exchange rate but that may have changed by the time you come to pay. Always allow a little in your calculations if you are buying in another currency than your own.

Action steps

Find out the products that you may want to sell and work out all the pricing and cost elements that go into the process. Once you have a unit cost (that is the cost of selling one item) then you can cross-reference this against what the rest of the market is selling on Amazon. Make sure that you can turn a good profit on the item and that

PHASE 2- HOW TO GET THE PRODUCT MADE FOR YOUR BRAND

Once you have an idea of what you want to sell then you will need to look at the net step of having that product developed and produced by someone. This is a really important part of the process because price and quality can vary between supplier so make sure that you find the right on that can get you what you and your customers want at a price that allows you to make money.

Contacting suppliers

There are many places that you can source suppliers (as I have mentioned so far threw website alibaba is a great place to start) and you will find them in business directories online or advertising their services online as well. Many of these are based in China and are used to dealing with buyers from all over the world and their English is very good too. Look through the directories or websites to find a supplier of the products that you want to sell. Each website will have contact details and you should use these official channels to get in touch with people as you want to be able to track what you are doing and know as best you can that you are dealing with a legitimate company. You may well be parting with quite a bit of your hard-earned money to these people so you want to know that they won't disappear with it when they are based on the other side of the world.

Ordering samples

You will want samples of the product that you are ordering from your supplier so that you can vouch for the quality of the products and fully know that these are what you and your customers are expecting. Again these suppliers are well versed in dealing with buyers from all over the world so you won't be asking them for something that they have never been asked before. You may have to pay a small fee or shipping charge for a sample but don't be put off by this. It is a small price to pay to ensure that you will be giving your customers a product that you will be proud to sell and that you know you can confirm the quality of. Too many sellers try to save a little money here and end up not knowing exactly what it is they are selling. This is a dangerous way to operate and you may come unstuck if you start to receive customer complaints and have no way of going back to your supplier to query what they have delivered. Your reputation forms a large part of your presence on Amazon FBA as your products and you receive feedback ratings. You want to control your online reputation as best you can and by knowing what you are having delivered to your customers you know that you can rest assured.

You may get a product sample and find that it is not up to the standards that you require. Don't be afraid to go back to your supplier and get any issue resolved at this stage. You are dealing with professional business people and they would rather know about a problem and have the chance to resolve it. Treat all of your transactions in a professional and businesslike manner and you will get the most out of your business.

Placing your order

Once you have found your supplier, you are satisfied that you can make a profit from your product and you have received a sample that you are happy with then you can place an order. The contract that you sign with the supplier will be legally binding so make sure that you have read it thoroughly and that you understand all that it entails. The most important part is the payment terms so you must know when you are to pay for your products and when you should expect your Amazon fulfillment center to receive them. This is when the sales start to come in and you can start to make some money. If you are unsure about anything when it comes to placing the order then seek the help of a solicitor that has knowledge of international trade. You may be able to find one locally and you will definitely be able to find one on the internet. Have the contract checked out and make sure that you are protected from any unscrupulous operators when it comes to handing over your money and your signature.

There are often minimum order quantities with suppliers or price breaks when you get to a certain order levels so take a careful look at these and consider how many units you can sell before you commit to placing a large order. As part of your research you will have got a good idea about how many units you think you might be able to sell so use that information here to help you make the right decision.

PHASE 3 - HOW TO SET YOUR PRODUCT UP FOR SALES

Once you have ordered your products from the supplier of choice then there is still work to do. You want your product to launch with a bang and the best way to do this is to spread the word. Get that message out to as many people as possible and get your new product in their eye line.

Building a launch list

Your product will launch on a particular date. That will be a day or two after it arrives in the Amazon fulfillment center ready to be distributed to your customers and your money starts to roll in. But it is not a case of placing your order with a supplier and then having some down time until the launch date. This is valuable time and you need to make the most of it. This time is when you get to work on getting the word out there and building a list of customers that are just waiting to get their hands on your product when it is ready to go. Social media is a great and free tool to build your brand, create a level of excitement and get the word out there. You can use your social media accounts to tell people about the product and start to explain some of the features and benefits that make it stand out from the crowd. This is time really well spent while your supplier is busy manufacturing and shipping your new product. If you have a few samples from the selection process then it is a good idea to get reviews of your product from friends, family or relevant reviewers to enhance the way it is received when it is finally available for your customers to purchase.

Creating blogs or having others bloggers feature your product is another way to get great exposure for your up and coming product that will available to buy soon. Find relevant bloggers that will have readers that could be potential buyers for your item. Perhaps, again if you have samples, to give away a product or two as part of a feature, promotion or competition. Anything that engages people with your product and gives you a chance to build up a launch list will help you when it comes to gaining sales. Many Amazon categories will allow people to pre-order so the more people that you can get to the order page the better it is for you. Imagine a situation where you have started to sell a large proportion of your stock before it even arrives at the Amazon fulfillment center! This is a great way to do business and give you the opportunity to continue this process by re-ordering from your supplier and re-marketing your product all over again. The longer you can keep up this cycle of pre-orders the better it is for your business because you free up your capital sooner and it allows you to get that next batch of your great product on the production line and then into the shipping containers.

Creating and optimizing your listings

The way that your listing looks, feels and sounds makes a huge difference to how you make sales. Remember back to when we looked at Privet Labels products and how you can make your own product and gain greater sales by differentiating an almost identical product from your competition. The key to all of this is the way that your product is described and optimized.

When you set up a product listing with Amazon there are several key areas that you enter information yourself to create something that hopefully finds the right buyers and encourages them to part with their money. But just having a listing on Amazon is not enough. You need to have the right listing that contains the right words to attract the right buyers.

The mains areas that you need to consider are the product title, product description and product category. It is the words that you enter into the first two fields and the decision that you make with the third that will determine the success or otherwise of the product that you are trying to sell. The product title is the thing that most people will see and is the part of the information you have entered that will help Amazon to match a search term from a potential customer to you and your product. For example if someone searches for "noise cancelling microphone" and that is what your product dopes then you will need to make sure that you have those exact words in your product title. This will allow you to appear as high as possible in the searches and be found by your customers. Make sure that all the fields and niches are covered by your description because Amazon allows for a lot of characters in the product title. If your product covers several niches then try to mention them all or at least the important ones.

The product description file comes into play when your customer has found your product in a search. It is the wording that will persuade your customer to buy. Once they have found your product in search they want to know what it does, how it fills their need and why it is different to the others they could buy in Amazon. This is where your marketing and descriptive skills need to come to the fore because you can convert viewers of your page into buyers of your product. Think about what message you want to convey and the way that you will persuade people to click on the "buy" button. You want your words to accurately describe the ways in which your product is better than all the rest and get your customer to believe that they are making the right decision in committing to buy from you. Work hard at this and make sure that you get it right. It is heartbreaking to generate loads of interest from your product title and then for the product description to let you down.

Brainstorming potential reviewers

Amazon carries a list of the top reviewers on their site. These are the people that have gotten the most helpful votes on the reviews that they have submitted. Helpfully Amazon includes this list for you to browse and even more helpfully each reviewer gives you an idea of the type of products they like to review and often a contact email address. This means that you can look through the list and get an idea of the people that may be able to help you. Be prepared for a lot of rejection because these reviewers will get a lot of emails but if you ask nicely, include a compelling reason to review and offer to send them one of your samples then you may get a review from one of the influential people on the Amazon website. This allows you to start to build a set of reviews as early in the life of your product as possible. The beauty of Amazon is that is gives peers the chance to exchange their opinion and experiences of a product. The better reviews and the more of them then the more a product is trusted by potential buyers. If a buyer cannot differentiate between products on description and price then the review will make a massive difference to their buying choice. By having the right reviewers take a look at your product and share their experience you give it the best chance of finding the right market.

PHASE 4 - HOW TO LAUNCH YOUR PRODUCT FOR THE MOST IMPACT

As your product launches you want it to make as big a splash as possible to generate interest and sales for you. It is important to keep up the impact that you created from your pre-launch activity because this is the time when you need to convert interest into sales. There are a few ways of keeping your product in the limelight at this important time.

Getting initial reviews

As I have already said, reviews are really important when it comes to getting our product seen and trusted. And this is the key word here – trust. Potential buyers want to know that your product has been well received by others and that it will do what they want it to do. So you need to push for reviews. There are sites that offer reviews for a fee but let me point out that this is against the policies and procedures of Amazon so you really should avoid these.

Once a buyer has purchased your product then you will be able to contact them to ask for a review. If you explain that it is a new product and you want to know what people think of it in a nice and polite manner then you will be likely to get some reviews for your product. Anything here that builds up the picture of how people are using your product and what they think of it will allow you to find more buyers. This is because they will now have a better picture of what people think of your product. Encourage friends and family to buy your product and leave a review because this all adds up to a better chance of making sales.

Using a giveaway to generate initial sales

You can give some of your product away to generate interest and reviews for the product in the early days. It gets the product out there, gets the name out there and will generate reviews that will more often than not be really positive about what you have given away. If someone receives something for free then they will be more likely to be happy with it and will tell their friends and family through social media so you get extra exposure for your product and the Amazon listing. This is a great way to get people to engage with what you have to offer and be excited about your product. Where you increase the opinion of your new product with people then you have a greater chance of making more sales. This is especially relevant if you are selling a consumable product that someone may buy more than one of in a year. By giving them the first one for free they will be likely to return and buy a second when they need one.

Follow up with buyers to get feedback

Get in touch with your buyers whenever you can to see how they are getting on with your product. Even if it does not lead to feedback rating on the Amazon website it gives you an idea of how things are going and allows you to make any changes with your next order with your supplier if you need to. The feedback may be related to the packaging, the instructions or the product itself but every piece of information that you can gather helps you to build up a picture that gives you the ability to alter your product or the description you have on Amazon. Always seek information from people because your future business may depend on it.

PHASE 5 - HOW TO PROMOTE YOUR PRODUCT TO KEEP YOUR SALES UP

You want to keep up the promotion of your product all year round. Once the initial, excitement has died down it can be difficult to know what to do to get more buyers. But don't worry the answers are iout there, in fact the answers are next-

Ads (fb, google, twitter, instagram etc.)

There are many ways of gaining exposure to new markets with the internet. The fact that your product suits on Amazon 34 hours a day, 7 days a week every week of the year is a great help and means that it can find buyers for you while you concentrate your efforts elsewhere. But it isn't always enough, especially if you want to turn this from a one-off to a real business that can change your life.

As with the pre-launch there is a great deal that social media can do for you. It is initially a free tool to find new market, new buyers and to generate more sales. But sometimes your social media efforts need a little push and this is where adverts can come in really useful. Facebook, Twitter and the other main social media platforms allow you to advertise your products on there to people that you may not have been able to reach yourself. You specify the location of the people who receive the advert as well as being able to control some other factors and you set a budget of how much per day you want to spend. This budget can be low to fit into any expenditure restraints that you may have. It gives you access to relevant customers and is what is known as target advertising, because it allows you to choose the parameters of the people you want to see the advert.

Reddit (forums in general etc)

There are many forums where you can submit an image of your product, the details of your product or the link the Amazon product page and other users will vote on it. It gives you another outlet to get exposure for your product and have people talking about it and sharing it. Any way in which you can get exposure for your product and encourage people to talk about it helps you to keep up the interest levels and potentially find new customers that hadn't been aware of it before.

There are also press release websites where you can submit a press release that gives details about the product and a link to your product page. Again it is another way of finding new markets and new customers that may have a need for your product but just haven't found it yet.

There has been a lot to take in with this chapter but I hope that the overriding messages were to do your research and never stop working at gaining positive exposure for your product, There are billions of consumers in the world and there are many ways of finding people through the internet so keep on trying and you will find that the more people you tell about your product, the more sale you will get.

CHAPTER 7

10 HOT NICHES YOU CAN GET STARTED IN RIGHT NOW!

There are tens of millions of products available for sale on Amazon so it can be really hard to know where to start. I said earlier in the book that it can be a great idea to start with products that you know something about and you are passionate about. You will be spending a lot of time promoting these products so it is a good idea that they are something you can show a passion for in your promotion efforts. But that isn't always possible. The things that you may be knowledgeable and passionate about may be over-represented on Amazon or you just may not be that passionate about any of the products available to you. But don't worry if this is the case. I am here to help you with ideas about where you could start when it comes to selling on Amazon with the FBA program to make money and create a business that earns for you all year round. Here are my 10 hot niches you can get started in right now-

1. **Arts and crafts.** This is a popular and growing niche. People love to spend their spare time in creating things with their hands and you will find a huge market for this on Amazon. It is also easy to find a supplier and get a great Private Label product for your market in this area. Take a look at the section on Amazon and you will find everything from stencils to projects book, from stickers to glue. There are many possibilities for the Private Label seller to make a great FBA profit on Amazon.

2. **Kitchenware.** This is another great place to start with a Private Label FBA business because there is so much scope. You can have products manufactured in China and have a huge mark-up on what you can get for them in your own territory. You can easily change the branding and

logo and sell as a local product on Amazon to appeal to your local market. There are kitchen utensils, tableware and various other kitchen gadgets that can make you a goof living on Amazon if you select the right products and market them in the right way.

3. **Home Improvement**. There is a massive market for home improvement in many ways. People are always looking to make their home better and spend an absolute fortune on these products. The competition here has always been the home improvement stores such as Home Depot but you can easily undercut these with a Private Label product, open up the market with an Amazon listing and describe them in a compelling way that will bring you in sales. Home improvement is a really huge area so you will need to do your research before settling on a product.

4. **Camera accessories**. This is another growing area that you can tap into with a Private Label and an FBA account. People spend a lot of money on a camera and then they spend a lot of money on looking after it and getting the most from it. You can get these made a low cost and then have them shipped straight out to start selling on Amazon. Think camera bags and other accessories to get the most from this niche market.

5. **Baby accessories**. Babies are big business. People will spend every last penny they have to make sure that their baby is comfortable, clean and happy. The fact is that people love their babies and want to give them everything that they can. When it comes to this niche you want to think about bibs, bandanas, shower hats and hair bands. This market is massive and you can tap into it if you find the right product at the right price for your customers.

6. **Bike accessories**. This is something else that people love to spend their money on. When the average price for a

cycle is around $670 then you know that these consumers will also spend big on keeping that bike in top condition. They want it to look good and they want to cycle safely. Make sure that you know what people are looking for and deliver it to them with a great description that appeals to their sense of adventure and safety. Bike lights are a great place to start but there is so much more out there to find sales from.

7. **Photo frames**. This is something else that is linked to the camera category and there is a push back again to traditional photo frames as people realize that keeping their photos in digital format makes it difficult for them to get the best use of a photo. You can get great photo frames at great prices from suppliers all over the world and make these look and feel personal to you and your market. Your customers will just love these if you can get the design and the branding right. This is an area of high competition but don't be afraid to get in this market if you have an eye for a great product and the ability to make it stand out from the crowd.

8. **Cell phone accessories.** This is a competitive market but can be a lucrative one if you get things right. This is where you need to get your product reviews in as soon as possible to stand out from the crowd. If you find the right things such as screen protectors and cell phone camera attachments then you will be able to gain a loyal following and sell in bulk. These are often low value items though so you will need to sell a lot of these items to make your money. This is when FBA really comes into its own because you have the two advantages of someone else dealing with the shipping and access to the Amazon Prime market of customers.

9. **Flashlights and lanterns.** There is a steady market for these and with the different bran ding option sit is easy to

be able to make your product stand out from the crowd. In days gone by people bought a torch or flashlight and it lasted them for their life. But now with products becoming replaced every few years there will always be a market for these products. There are so many options when it comes to color, size, battery size and branding that you can easily produce something that looks very different to everything else that the market offers on Amazon.

10. **Alternative health items.** People want to look after themselves and the different ways that this can be done offer you a great market to tap into with your Private Label products. Alternative or non-medical health products are another big market niche because consumers want to look after themselves in as natural and non-invasive way as possible. Mosquito repellent bracelets and travel sickness bands are just two of the options in this area as people look to Amazon for the solutions to problems like these.

This is by no means an exclusive or exhaustive list but these are niches that you can investigate and get selling in within a matter of weeks. When it comes to selling then you want to just get on with the right product and start to bring in the money. This is why I have included this list here so you can have places to begin and just get on with your business. Do your research, select your products, find your supplier and get them sent to you. It can be as easy as this.

CONCLUSION

Amazon FBA is a great way to set up a business and make good money from the products that you sell on there. You need to get everything together and set it up right to get the most out of the FBA program and this book gets you on the right track with this. As we have talked you through all the steps you need to take in order to be a success on the Amazon FBA program I hope that it has inspired you to be the next successful entrepreneur on the website. And that is what I want for you. This book puts it all into perspective and allows you to follow a successful process that can get you the business you want. The idea is that you can follow all of the steps that I have outlined and turn an idea into a business that makes you money every week of the year. This is something that can set you up for life if you work it right.

Amazon is a place where people go to get the items they want. But when you use FBA in the right way, Amazon is a place that people go when they want to get rich. If you find the right product and present it in the right way then you can become one of these people. Amazon, FBA and this book can give you the business you desire in a much shorter space of time that you probably realized. Now that you have the tools to become successful then wait no longer. Get off your ass and make a success of it!

Selling on Amazon is something that can be done and done successfully by anyone. If you have an eye for a product then all the much better but even without this eye for a product then there is enough information out there to be able to pull together all you need to find a winner. As you do this over and over again you will get better at the process and find that you are able to predict sales with an accuracy that you would not believe possible at the start. When you add this information to the ability to Private Label a product then you are maximizing your earning potential. Private Labeling eliminates all of the direct competitors from your product page and makes you the only seller. If you get your description, branding and logos just right then you become the seller of choice for the millions of Amazon customers. Add to this the power of being an FBA seller and you multiply this advantage again. FBA gives you access to the lucrative and active Amazon Prime market where the customers have already paid an annual fee for their shipping so you have the advantage that they choose your product and Amazon does all the hard work of picking, packing and shipping for you. There really is no better way to do business. This frees you up to do all the interesting stuff like finding the next product, negotiating with the suppliers and doing all the marketing. This is a much better life than picking products and travelling backwards and forwards to the post office all day long.

Use this book in the way that it was meant. It is here to provide you with inspiration and instruction on how to turn an idea into a great Amazon FBA business that generates you great money all the time.

I wish you all the luck in the world with your business and I hope to be reading about you in the industry press in the future as a successful Amazon FBA seller that has made it big.

CAN I ASK A FAVOUR?

If you enjoyed this book, found it useful or otherwise then I'd really appreciate it if you would post a short review on Amazon. I do read all the reviews personally so that I can continually write what people are wanting.

If you'd like to leave a review then please go ahead and visit the Amazon product page

Thank you for your support!

BONUS #1

Tips to Starting Your Own Kindle Publishing Business

As a token of my appreciation for purchasing this book, I have decided to add an additional chapter which I think will immensely help you to get started with your own publishing business. As always don't forget to rate and comment and tell me how you liked this book!

TIP 1: PICK YOUR NICHE

When choosing a topic for your book, find a niche that's large enough to generate sufficient sales, while still small enough that you can dominate it. To identify such a niche, generate a list of keywords that best describes your own expertise and then search for books on those topics in the Kindle Store. Stick to UK versions if your book will mainly appeal to natives, otherwise base your analysis on Amazon.com. Start with quite a broad search phrase and narrow it whenever you encounter too many competitors.

For example, you might start by searching for plain "Raspberry Pi" if you're interested in writing about this cheap computing phenomenon.

Sort your results by popularity and then open the top one. When I tried this it was, hardly surprisingly, the official Raspberry Pi User Guide (co-written by Gareth Halfacree of this parish). Its ranking at just over 5,000 suggests sales of at least 15 copies per day at a royalty of £6 per copy, or some £90 per day, £30,000+ per annum from UK sales. Not bad.

Repeat this process by moving down the search list. In this example, the second-most popular title generates around £22 per day and the next few £16, £5 and £2.50 respectively. You'll notice a familiar pattern here, where two-thirds of the revenues go to the most popular title and more than 80% to the top two together. Carry on down some way and you'll very soon be among books that required considerable effort to produce but are selling around one copy a week.

You conclude that there's clearly money to be made from an enthusiastic audience eager to learn, especially considering that you've only looked at UK Kindle sales so far, and many of these titles will be available globally in multiple formats. But you also see plenty of titles in this niche that have failed to make any impact at all.

TIP 2: PUBLISH A GREAT BOOK

Having located your market niche, you'll need to produce the goods. Remember to closely base your actual title on the keywords you researched, since this is how your audience will find you on Amazon. This may sound obvious, but if you were to compare the best-selling books in any particular category with those that languish in the virtual equivalent of a box under the bed, you'll notice big differences in quality – the most popular books will be professionally presented, complete and well written.

Having a copy editor run through your book at least once before publishing is an excellent investment, and unless you're a graphic artist you should also hire a cover designer. Many potential readers get no further than the thumbnail, and since the ebook shops don't separate titles into ones published by industry giants and home-produced efforts, your "Guide to Microsoft Office" needs to look the business when viewed alongside similar titles from the big guns.

Fortunately, neither copy-editing nor cover design are particularly expensive: just make sure you pick contractors who are qualified and competent, rather than automatically plumping for the cheapest.

Your book will succeed or fail based on the reviews it receives, so producing a professional package will go a long way to satisfying the fickle ebook audience.

TIP 3: GET THE PRICE RIGHT

Professor Brian Cox discovered just how fickle ebook purchasers can be when he contributed to a book that explains how the universe will end. This was part of a series called "Shorts", and managed to distil a complex subject down into an understandable format for 99p. The problem according to most Amazon reviewers was that he did this in a measly 20 pages. You might think having the end of the universe explained in layman's terms for less than a quid is a bargain, but many Kindle readers disagreed, measuring value based purely on pages per penny.

The rules of print paperback production don't apply to ebooks

This said, the rules of print paperback production don't apply to ebooks, since readers can't judge a Kindle book by its heft in their hand – anything above about 50 pages will usually be considered a reasonable read for a non-fiction book.

When you plan your book, then, consider the right size. I planned to sell my 200-pager for £4.99, but it might have been wiser to split it into four 50-page chunks on different aspects of the topic, then sell each for £1.49. This will work better for some subject matter than others; just remember that the ebook format frees you from any specific page count.

Once your book has been released, experiment with pricing. Mine has dropped from £4.99 at launch to a current price of £1.99. I left it at the high price for a few months, then tested the way changes affect revenue by dropping it to £1.49 over Easter, and finally raised it a little again. Surprisingly, I make much the same money from the book whatever its price, since roughly when I halve the price I double sales. But higher sales bring a better ranking and more reviews, both of which increase credibility and conversion rate, so while the revenue stream may be the same either way, I'd expect sales to last longer at a lower price point.

Tip 4: Multiple media

Writers and publishers have barely started breaking free of the constraints imposed by traditional printing methods, and I expect to see a lot of innovation in connecting together different media over the next few years. Our mythical Raspberry Pi book, for example, might contain links to supporting YouTube tutorials that show how to translate the principles it describes into practice.

For now, one effective way to maximize the return on your writing is to also publish your ebook as a paperback. Print-on-demand services such as Lulu and Amazon's own CreateSpace enable you to offer a paperback version, which can be delivered as quickly as a traditionally published book, since Amazon keeps a small stock. Actually, to Amazon there's no difference between a Lulu-printed book and one from HarperCollins, which regrettably means that it will take the same big chunk of its cover price.

On the other hand, linking your paperback and Kindle book together will drive sales of both, since reviews are amalgamated into a single listing that inevitably makes the ebook look a bargain.

You can also buy copies of your own print book at cost (around £3 each for a 200-page paperback) to sell directly through your own channels, which enables you to keep a much larger slice of the profit. Also consider offering a PDF version of the book direct from your own website, whose cost to you is close to zero.

TIP 5: FIND AN AUDIENCE

It isn't enough to write an excellent book, publish it and hope for the best. If you've done your research and picked a good title, some readers searching on Amazon will certainly find you, but you need to supplement them with direct traffic from other sources if you're to make the most of your hard work. One approach is to sell your book directly as I just mentioned: if you have an established website with an appropriate audience, consider both selling the printed version and including links to the Kindle version.

You can also tap an existing community for valuable marketing information. I asked the customers of my retail craft business what they wanted covered in my book and was surprised by their replies: my book was all the better for their direct input. I promised a free copy of the ebook to all who contributed, then emailed to ask for their reviews once they'd read it. Frankly I was disappointed by that response, as the 100 contributors wrote only a couple of reviews between them. For my next book I'll be looking at strategies for getting more reviews that are available on publication day, since these strongly influence sales.

Google+ recently introduced "Communities", a feature that allows like-minded people to discuss related topics in a far more sophisticated manner than Facebook's Pages or Groups. If you were writing a book about, say, Raspberry Pi, there are several communities devoted to that device you can join – contribute to them and you earn the right to gently promote your book from time to time.

My experience was that income from KDP Select lending outstripped combined revenues from the Apple, Barnes & Noble and Kobo stores

Communities are also a great place to learn more about your subject – including self-publishing itself (check out the APE:

Authors, Publishers, Entrepreneurs) – particularly in fast-moving fields. I think Communities may prove to be the killer feature of Google+, with much of the social network's interaction taking place in these super-forums. I'll also be more actively building an email list for my next book – which, after all, is what I'd do for any other product or business.

TIP 6: STICK TO ONE PLATFORM

This one's simple: don't bother with any other ebook platform until you've nailed Kindle Direct Publishing (KDP). Even then, think carefully about whether your time will be well spent – I've described previously the tortuous hoops I was put through to get my title published on Apple's iBookstore, Barnes & Noble's Nook and the Kobo store. That was an utter waste of time I could otherwise have spent either promoting sales on KDP or writing another book.

Perhaps I shouldn't have been so surprised since – in the case of Apple's devices – readers have the option to use the Kindle app rather than iBooks. The market for Nook and Kobo books seems tiny compared with that for Kindle, and I'd only bother if you've exhausted all avenues to increase sales on Amazon's platform.

Sticking exclusively to KDP qualifies your title for the KDP Select program, which enables you to offer your book free for a specified number of days in order to drum up interest and generate reviews. Perhaps more significantly still, it means your ebook can be borrowed by Kindle-owning members of Amazon's Prime program. You'll be paid each time someone borrows your book, and while the amount isn't huge (around £1 per loan), my experience was that income from KDP Select lending outstripped combined revenues from the Apple, Barnes & Noble and Kobo stores.

TIP 7: ONE NICHE, MULTIPLE TITLES

I haven't tested this tip yet, but I've come across it many times during my research. It makes sense that if a reader likes your book they may well enjoy other books by you – but only so long as they cover a similar topic. This works with fiction too: I'd buy anything by Terry Pratchett within the genre for which he's famous, but if he published a book of romantic fiction I'd be off like a shot.

If your interests are too wide to accommodate within one genre, then take another tip from fiction and consider using a pen name for your other titles. However, from a business point of view, you ought to stick to a single niche, allowing you to offer book bundles, and even give away the first title in a series to drive sales of the rest. You can also cross-promote books, and the more titles you have, the more effective this will be.

Using these tips, I've made more money (both in revenue and profit) from one book over three months than from my entire stable of mobile apps in a year, and with far less time invested. Not surprisingly, then, I'll be experimenting further with self-publishing for profit over the coming year, and will keep you up to date.

BONUS #2

HOW TO MARKET YOUR KINDLE EBOOKS

The elementary principles of marketing and promotion are pretty much identical for an e-book as for a tangible book. When marketing e-books, it's ideal to do it online. There are quite a few nice strategies to assist you in this extremely important process.

Pricing makes a huge difference. Having a general understanding of what is actually selling in the market helps to make sure you're reasonably within the competitive range.

Here are the average prices of various kinds of works on Amazon:

- The average price of a hardcover book on Amazon is about $9.99
- Books that are on the market as trade soft covers often are priced from $5.99 to $7.99 as the Kindle editions
- Big market paperbacks generally cost around $2.99-$4.99
- Monthly subscriptions to magazines and newspapers are within the range of $9.99$14.99
- One magazine issue is within the $1.49-$2.99 range
- Some big name magazines are about ½ price of offline subscriptions
- Blog monthly subscriptions are about $0.99 with a typically free 14-day trial
- Articles that are by themselves and other short form works are $0.99-$2.99

How to Choose a Price

Theoretically, the lower the price on a book, the higher the conversion rate should be. Similar to selling products on websites, people have to know that your site exists as the first step; you can have the most sophisticated, creative, and high quality site out there, but if people have no idea it exists, what good is it? This concept works identically with e-books.

Here are some pricing tips for works you're selling:

- For diminutive length stories or works or articles, price it from $0.99 to $2.99
- For books, start low and change as needed
- It is highly suggested to not charge more than $9.99 for a usual novel-length book
- Softcover books should run from $2.99-$7.99
- Books only available in digital form should be priced with good judgment
- Depending on the niche your book is in, it may get by with being more expensive than the standard price; usually, these kinds of books deal with something very scientific, are saturated with a lot of graphics, or may be justified if you have to reimburse people who helped with the work.

Amazon Sales Rank

Amazon shows how great a work is performing via the sales ranking system. It's modified by the hour and is computed based on current and past sales information. In order to thin down a product's sales results, items are graded by how great they are performing in their solo niches with category sales ranks.

Standard sales rank is different because it displays how great a product is selling as a big picture. Only writers publishing via the KDP can see their sales reports in their own accounts.

How Sales Rank Works

The more people purchase your product in the Kindle store, the higher chances your work will become very recognizable in your niche. The more sales you make, the more exposure your work will get. It will be difficult to make it to the top ten, but even if you make it to the top 100 or even 500, your exposure and sales will enhance tremendously.

Customer reviews hold a high significance on book sales; poor reviews usually decrease book sales and positive reviews are the prerequisite to people telling their friends, family, and acquaintances about how great your work was, meaning a lot more sales!

Transitioning into paper books

If it happens that you decide to release a title solely for the Kindle but later put forward a Print on Demand edition of that book, the sale information and review assessments for the e-book edition diffuse into the print version that is sold in the standard Amazon book store section of the site.

To ensure the formatting of your book is pleasant in the Print on Demand version, check out CreateSpace; to find it online, just put in "createspace" in the Amazon search bar to pull it up. **CreateSpace** is a supplementary company to Amazon. When you see the page, it'll allow you to register and submit works for no charge.

When you make a Print on Demand title, CreateSpace gives a free ISBN if you don't have it at the time of registering. After you acquire this number, you may use it for your current Kindle title so that the two will be connected together on Amazon.

Promotions

There are a multitude of methods to promote your eBook. Here are some strategies to use in introducing your new work:

- It is ideal, since you're a new author and have to prove yourself to your audiences, to start with a cheap introductory price like $0.99. After your book picks up the pace in sales and become trendier, you can increase the price slowly as time goes on.

- If you have a long length book, it is worth a shot to put up a small excerpt of it as being available for sale as a teaser that will persuade readers to purchase the book in its whole form. If you have a non-fiction book, you can pull out a small section of content that is very helpful, abstract, and/or not well known.

If you wrote a fiction book or other fiction based work, take an excerpt from a very exciting part of the book where it's from an escalated action point or some other highlight. The bottom line is that whatever people read in the excerpts showcased, should really incite a strong desire to read the rest of it. Excerpts run from $0.99-$2.49 and are about the length of an article from 1-5 pages.

Serializing Your Work

If you have a work (non-fiction or fiction) that is very lengthy, it's a good idea to chop it up into sections and sell them apart from each other. As a guideline, think of novelettes from about 7,000-18,000 words; novellas from around 18,000-40,000 words; books/novels as 40,000+ words.

The most important point to remember is that in your series, every chapter should be able to stand on its own "two legs," meaning that the end of the chapter should leave a cliffhanger where it begs the reader to want to read the next chapter. The Charles Dickens' books are an example of successful serialized series.

It's up to you if you prefer to finish the work completely and then start serializing it, or if you prefer to write it as you progress. After your e-book is serialized from beginning to end, you may publish it as one volume. Taking the approach of serializing can be beneficial for the promotion of your work because it can build up curiosity and eagerness while creating a flame around the series.

All of these traits can assist in wheeling in new readers. If your work qualifies as bringing in the heat to readers, it might be able to mainly rely on people telling others about it and social marketing advertisement.

Press Release

Putting out a press release may be worth a shot to include in your marketing portfolio; it could help market your e-book mainly if you're a resident in a small to medium sized city. This may help because you would be a local resident publishing a book, which may be considered exciting and attention-grabbing.

Your home-based radio stations, newspapers, and television channels might become interested in an article or interview; this exposure would be just what you need to market your book in your town. Be very methodical in choosing the newspapers or television stations you'll target by doing research on them to see if what you will offer will have a higher chance of creating interest to that station.

For example, if you are writing a book about how weather affects people's moods and health, choosing weather stations to target would be a logical decision. Don't just pick and submit to many stations without doing your homework. It is a good idea to write a cover letter to a specific person with a press release or phone call.

How to Social Network Offline

To network efficiently means to keep an eye and ear open to latest opportunities. Try your best to make the most of what opportunity comes your way, meaning how you can advertise your work in your community and in other avenues.

It is helpful to start by looking at the topic your work is about to choose where it could fit, i.e. If your work is regarding the history of reptiles, you could see if there are any zoos, aquariums, and museums in your area to tell your book about. There could also be an animal appreciation group that might be interested in promoting your e-book.

If you're a newcomer to the sport of publishing, you might want to read industry works similar to your genre, i.e. if your niche is in healthy food, check out reading magazines such as Cooking Light and other related publications so you can be familiar with similar groupings and organizations.

You could take an extract from your work and send an article to them as well. If your article is approved and published, you can request the editor to put a note that the article is selected from your Kindle book, and tag on the title and a url to the work. Be open minded with trying various ideas and always be on the lookout for promoting opportunities.

Relatives and Friends

It can't be stressed enough how important it is to let as many people know about your book via word of mouth. You just never know how its influence can affect your work immensely. Let your family and friends know all about it via a well written email! They have contacts that they can send the email to and a snowball effect can happen.

Business Contacts and Professional Groups

It's a good idea to converse with your professional associates and co-workers when it's fitting to do so; a great idea is to throw a festival to rejoice in the introduction of your Kindle work. Invite workers to the party who have a matching interest to your work's topic. Think about visiting conferences with your work's industry alliances.

Take a couple of tangible copies of your book or a paper ad for your Kindle version to give out to people. Keep in mind that you should be very cautious about how you approach this kind of advertising while conversing with people. You should NOT be very pushy and force your work on anyone; it's considered unprofessional and this act could backfire and give you a horrible reputation—think of it like a website being designated as spam.

The key is to time when and how to act, i.e. if you trade contact information with an editor or publisher, be sure to contact them again in a suitable amount of time and write a sophisticated kind of letter that reminds them of your meeting so you can make sure they remember the correct person. Visit a few conferences if possible. Be vigilant in your networking and learning more data.

You may also get more involved by volunteering in some conferences; you can assist in planning one or put on your creative thinking caps and participate in some other form for a professional society. By doing this, you will get "brownie points" and not be ignored for your efforts, thus helping your reputation.

If you're timid, you are going to have to realize that you have to put yourself out there. Think of it like acting. Practice acting to help ease into the process. It may help you out first to start assisting with things that need it at first to ease yourself into it. Speak to people and trade business cards when the chance happens.

Professional Image

Two groups that are great for published writers to join because they supply a multitude of professional related assets are PEN and The Author Guild. The Author's Guild supports different and important issues for published authors like law-based services, rights' protection, and just reimbursement.

A part of this membership's obligation is that book authors must have a work from an American publisher that is reputable and who obtains a percentage of the work's sales with a large advance in which the writer is the copyright owner.

Unfortunately, if you only have a work on the Kindle, you don't qualify; however, if you signed a royalty contract on your Kindle work with a reputable American publisher that has offered a major advance, then you would meet the criteria. Bear in mind that this type of situation happening is very improbable. Other types of writers that may qualify are contributors, translators, coauthors, ghostwriters, and freelance writers.

PEN promotes open expression as its main foundation. According to its website, its members have published at least two books of "literary character or one book of exceptional distinction."

Here are some websites to some qualified societies that will help guide you:

- The Creative Penn: www.thecreativepenn.com
- John August Screenwriting Tips: http://johnaugust.com
- The Reading Edge Podcast: http://thereadingedge.com
- TeleRead: www.teleread.org ☐ PEN: www.pen.org
- The Authors Guild: www.authorsguild.org
- The Graphic Artists Guild: www.graphicartistsguild.org
- Publetariat: People Who Publish: www.publetariat.com

Blog Marketing

Remember that just having a mind blowing novel on Kindle does not mean you'll automatically be triumphant and become rich. After your publisher has verified your account and it's ready to go, then you'll have the ability to blog right from Author Central for free by checking out the Blog tab. You can blog using two different methods; one method is to go to the "Add an RSS feed" tab and put in the feed address, NOT the blog's address.

Or, you can click the Create a new post address and put in a fresh post straight to Amazon via the box that generates. To make an RSS feed using Blogger, visit your blog to sign in and click Customize at the top. Check that the "Layout" tab is chosen and go to the link "Add a Gadget." Next, include the "subscription links" tool to your blog.

Then, perform all the actions the directions state for initiating this process, which are easy as pie. This is the way to get a RSS subscription capacity included in your blog. To locate your RSS feed address, check out the blog subscription url, which is on your blog's home page.

Click on the url and find "posts;" then, choose how you want your feed to look in its layout from the options given. The next page will showcase your feed address in a url. Copy and paste this url in the proper box at Author Central to begin extracting your blog feeds into your Author Central account. There will be a note giving caution that it may take up to 24 hours for brand new posts to appear on your author page.

Videos

Amazon has a very cool feature that lets authors upload videos. Go to the "videos" tab to upload your work. The following formats are what is accepted to upload videos in: .wmv, .flv, .mpg, .mov, and .avi. A huge advantage to putting up a video on your author page would be for credibility and helping to subtly market your book, i.e. if you performed speaking expeditions, these will look great for your profile.

Another option would be to upload a video of yourself talking about your work without giving away too much to ruin it, the reasons for writing your work, and other things about your work that will incite excitement and suspense. There is something about seeing someone express their passion in "person" vs. on paper alone that allows the reader to absorb it as well.

Amazon permits files that are at the biggest 500 MB. You should go to the "content guidelines" url to check that your video meets the content qualifications. Making a video is not as complicated as it may sound because most new computers come with a built-in camera. Videorecording functions differ depending on the computer.

You can start by doing a search on your computer using the keywords "video" or "camera." If you don't have a camera built into your computer, then you can buy a latest webcam for as low as $8 from www.buy.com. You can also check out www.amazon.com to see if it has cheap webcams.

Cameras are diverse, so you should invest some time in reading the directions to learn how to set it up and record appropriately. Trust me; this'll save you a lot of heartache down the road if you just learn how to do it the right way from the start.

Take heed to the kinds of content Amazon does not allow to be posted:

- Obscene content or things that are offensive like nasty language or depicting other people in a bad way
- Promotions or advertisements
- Stuff that isn't yours to use
- Personal data like phone numbers, mailing addresses, and website urls
- Data on buying and shipping stuff, costs, and other things related
- Commentary to information that is accessible on your author page and within book reviews
- Promotions for good reviews and votes

- Plot spoilers (why would you want to do that anyway?!)

Happenings

After your account is ready to go, you'll be able to put facts regarding your speaking events, speeches, book tours, when you'll be in bookstores, and other happenings under the "events" tab. Amazon is a joint venture partner with a company called book tour: www.booktour.com They follow author occurrences, so all new events you put in your author central page will be distributed with Book Tour; book tour also gives your info to other sites/resources to give you further exposure.

To submit a new happening, go to the "create new event" section and input your description of the event, the location, the name of the work the event is correlated with, and the date and the time it'll begin. Make sure to be very specific and use loads of details as you can in the description section.

Definitely state if you'll be giving a speech on your book or similar topics because this will give you a wonderful chance to squeeze in advertising copy; the key is for it to be pertinent to the book and event bordering it. What you put in the description section needs to seduce readers into attending your event; events are a fabulous way to get exposure and demonstrate that you're involving yourself as a professional in the marketing of your work.

More on Blogs

Creating a name for yourself on the Internet is of vital importance. Amazon has a blog option as mentioned earlier, but it's relatively limited to the amount of exposure you can acquire than if you have a standard blog with one of the biggest free blog services on the net---WordPress and Blogger.

You can check these out by visiting:

http://wordpress.com

Or www.blogger.com

There is a big caveat to using a blog. You need to be honest with yourself and ask if you would want to keep posting to your blog at least once a week. A blog's main purpose is to give consistent updates and if you're not going to do that, there is no point in setting one up. It's simple to run a blog, so that's a good thing.

Here's an example of a fantastic blog by the author Anne Mini below. Read her biographic information as well to get an idea how some of these concepts stated in this book tie together. www.annemini.com. This blog contains an immense amount of helpful information that Anne wrote about grammar guidelines, manuscript layout help, and tons of other things dealing with editing, writing, and the ever evolving realm of publishing.

Your blog does not need to just focus only on your work; you can write about your experiences with your path to publishing for the Kindle, problems you may have ran into (more than likely, others can relate), overall experiences with e-publishing, marketing your work, and other various experiences with agents, editors, or publishers.

Other ideas for topics include writing about your specialize subject of comfort and a multitude of other experiences you have on a professional level of writing. Doing this will help you form a professional profile and reputation that will only enhance your future sales.

Website

Before thinking about investing funds into magazine advertisement, you should first invest money and time into a website instead. It's important to have one because so much information about yourself, works, etc can be put on there. It's ideal to have your website and blog all on one site, within the same domain name.

It is basically like your public identity as an author and a place that readers can easily check out for sources to things linked to your professional profile and work; it also helps that if someone wants to reach you that your contact info is on your site. You never want people to work too hard to be able to find you online because chances are that they will just give up and forget about it. Make it as easy as possible for people to find you online.

For some tips on what to put on your site, it helps to look at how others did it first to get an intuitive idea. It will be easiest just to hire a freelancer or friend to build one for you too on www.elance.com. Here are some useful links that can help give you a lot of ideas.

www.kevinprufer.com/index.html

www.mdbell.com

www.stephenking.com

www.how-to-build-websites.com/lessonOne.php

Suggested Information to Include on your website

- Cover graphics
- ISBN
- Summary of work
- Publication date
- Target readership
- Teaser excerpt from the first chapter
- Info about how and where to purchase your book (Make sure this is clear and easy to follow)
- Commentary of your works
- Summaries of each work you've published
- Promotional excerpts by other people in the business
- Don't interweave information; this means to separate your author biographic data from your personal or other non-

author career data. The exception is if your job relates to being an author, i.e. if you're a librarian.

- Put in future dates and a chart of previous events like lecture or book tours (that you've attended or are scheduled to attend) that occurred.

As a final reminder, it's very important to keep the material on your site fresh and update at least once a week. If you find yourself in a position to not have anything to think of writing, post news and events in the business from around the internet, or your feedback to a work you've read lately. Just be in the habit (which will put your readers in the habit of checking out your site) of doing this and it'll be easy to continue after a while.

Aside from keeping readers keeping up with what you're doing, it's vital to having a lot of content on your site because this will increase the number of other sites that will link to your site; this linking is very helpful in helping to rank your site in the search engines. Making a positive impression with Google can never hurt, since it's the biggest search engine at the moment.

Now, you have a great starting point to begin your quest to becoming an accomplished author on Kindle. There are many resources available to help. Go for it!

ABOUT THE AUTHOR

Craig Lebowski is a writer, author, entrepreneur, life coach, personal trainer, speaker and an avid traveler.

Craig has been making money online since 2013 and decided to hop on to Kindle and share with the world his wealth of knowledge. Craig loves the luxury of being able to travel and yet make money doing so.

He always tells his clients, you don't need to think of travelling as an expense but rather as an investment.

Some of his hobbies include:

- Meditation, Mindfulness and The Meaning of Life
- Running, Biking, Swimming, Rock Climbing
- Helping Individuals Reach Their Full Potential
- Spending Time With His Family
- Playing Competitive Basketball
- Writing, Traveling, Blogging

If you want to learn more about Craig or how to earn income online, you can go ahead and visit his blog (earnsixfigurenow.com).

www.ingramcontent.com/pod-product-compliance
Lightning Source LLC
Chambersburg PA
CBHW070227210526
45169CB00023B/1021